I0424447

In My Haitian State of Mind

In My Haitian State of Mind

Jean E. Pierre

Copyright © 2010 by Jean E. Pierre.

Library of Congress Control Number:		2010906502
ISBN:	Hardcover	978-1-4500-9768-0
	Softcover	978-1-4500-9767-3
	Ebook	978-1-4500-9769-7

All rights reserved. No part of this book may be reproduced or transmitted in any form or by any means, electronic or mechanical, including photocopying, recording, or by any information storage and retrieval system, without permission in writing from the copyright owner.

This book was printed in the United States of America.

To order additional copies of this book, contact:
Xlibris Corporation
1-888-795-4274
www.Xlibris.com
Orders@Xlibris.com
78440

CONTENTS

CHAPTER I

Unity

The solution to our entire problems is for us to come together in a unifying way as we did during slavery to have any chance of solve these crises in Haiti. The broken education system, the extreme poverty, and most importantly, the broken government system, are some of the many issues that are crippling our country at a fast rate. As you can see, these issues are very complex, so therefore, the road ahead for us is steep and challenging.

The Haitians people must know, in order to win any wars, you first have to know who your opponent is; and why you in a conflicts with your opponents, and what are you hoping to achieves from your opponents. As we will be coming together to solve these crises in Haiti as I mention above, our opponents is very clear to me. Sadly, to say, our opponents to achieve a better education system; reduce the gap between the rich and the poor; and last but not least to fix our broken government system is we. The question one might raise, how could that be? Why would any country would wanting to remain in a broken education system, why would any country would wanting to remain one of the poorest country in the world, and worse of all, why would any country would wanting to remain in a broken government system? Well, the answer is as simple as it has seemed to me. If a country is in a bad condition and the country does not do anything to improve the condition, the country agree with the condition, so therefore, the condition will continue to get worsen until the country have had enough. My assumption is, that Haiti have not reach it boiling point quite yet, as history showed when we do, we will revolt and prevail.

When we prevail, we will come together and fight for a better Haiti. Indeed, I have come to realize what most Haitians ever wanted sincerely is a better Haiti. A country that is safe for every single Haitians. A country that is unify in every way possible. A country that is promising to all of our children, from the day they were born through the day God call up on them. However, we must realize we will not achieve anything without being unifying as a country first, for the sake of the country. We must realize there is power in unity. If you have any doubt, you must look in the middle of our flag, and study the story behind of our flag. As we will prevail in the coming decades, we have to practice what we preach, which is "unity is power." (Lunion fait l'aforce). If you study the story of our flag bring about, you would realize the unity of our greatest generation of all time was the keystone reason for its stand. As you know the greatest generation of Haiti faced tremendous obstacles during their generation and have prevailed; since then, as we go through worthless generation after generation, every obstacles we have faced, have gotten us into more and deeper obstacles. It is saddening me that our slaves' leaders had more respect in the world then our present leaders would ever to dream. Those leaders did not have much of education. They were force to work free their entire lives. They beat them through the end of their life. They had no rights. They wives were being raped. They would take their children, sold it to different master, and worse of all, when they did not have enough strength to be slaves, they would force them to dig holes, buried them alive, and left their head out; then the master would get syrup dropped in their head for insect to have a feast while being alive. Winning these obstacles was not easy, our slaves leaders knew they was not going to be easy but they knew it was a fight they had to win and they did, despite losing one the greatest leader the world had ever seen, which goes by the name of Toussaint Louvereture. In fact, by even mention today leaders (if could called them that) in the same breath of our slave leaders is a slapped in the faced to our slave leaders even though they had many fault on their own. We may never have the same great leaders as we did during the slavery era, but I have no doubt in my mind that we will have great leaders again.

Since there are no leaders in Haiti, I will refer to them as people in power. Now, people in power are facing similar difficulties as our greatest generation faced during their generation; given that they are facing similar difficulties, any reasonable people in power would use the same or a better approach than our leaders did to prevail in their battles. One of the main thing they did successfully was unified the slaves. If our leaders could unify slaves, there should be no reason why our people whom in power cannot unify free people. With that in mind, the unity of the people was so deep during these obstacles, they stamped in the middle of our flag as a remembrance of our standing; "L'union fait la force".

If our people in power, follow the same strategy our leaders put in place for us during slavery, I have no doubt, we would have one of the best country in the world, because through unity, nothing is impossible for the Haitians people. As we unify as a country, the obstacles we are facing today will be history just as slave was in Haiti. While Haiti is becoming a country that is creating jobs for the Haitians people, the Haitian people will understand the price of job creation is to follow law and order. With jobs creation in Haiti, I believe the Haitian people will follow law and order. Beside our independence day and very few other occasions, history has proved the only time Haiti has united, is only in the time of destruction. Although that is true, what also more true, that we have had nothing through our history. I see these divisions as a sign of frustration for not having anything for past two centuries. These frustrations have made the country less safe and worse off. We have people in power in Haiti for the past two centuries, but what we need in Haiti are leaders. I hope in the next coming decades, as we unit to find solution for these obstacles in Haiti, I am extremely hopeful some leaders will evolve as well. It is widely prove to me that those in Haiti that is in power for century are seem to be clueless of what power is, because they keep following the same fail strategies for centuries.

As we will calling for unity in Haiti, the world will say to us, what other country that is solely black that are unify in the world. They will put doubt in the Haitians people. They will use their best weapons against us, which are to turn us against us. I am sadly to say some of us will fall for their trap; many of us will not. However, it will be our jobs to put that Haitians Judas, back to our side as we call for unity in Haiti. We will have one message and one voice as a nation, just as our leaders did during slavery, which was "give us freedom or give us death". Our message is going to be, we were the first black race to won the war against slavery in the western hemisphere, and we will be the first black race to practice unity in the world. As you could imagine, the world would feel threaten to see a black race come together for something greater than themselves. The world know when black people are unified for something greater than themselves, no white, yellow, red green, brown men can stand in their way. More than a few centuries ago, there were no cowards in Haiti, if we decided to put our mind in something as a nation, we get it or we die for it. I can only imagine the pride and the joys our fathers after the victory of slavery, I would give anything to live during these Haitians monument times. The time of unity is power (l'union fait force). My dream for Haiti, is two century later for some Haitian kids to reflect on my generation legacy, as I am reflected at the the end of the slave generation legacy. our generation, must do something special to end poverty in Haiti for the next generation of Haitians, if we don't, our existence will be in deeper trouble, and it might even be to late for any resurrection.

Many people would agree with me a quick death is better than a long prolong suffer death. We the Haitians people have been dying for a long time. I believe the time will come, when the Haitian people will stop destroying each other, rather come in a unifying way to help one a another as we ought to be. I am well aware by being an advocate for a better Haiti; I will be the target of so many. For he or she that will be taking my life, I hope to meet you in heaven, as I am praying for God to bless your soul; as for my faith, I asking God forgiveness in the sky for knowing what may happened to my life and yet I still continue with my mission. However, for a better Haiti, God is my witness; I would want to be the first in line to meet my death in return for a better Haiti. As we all know, death is inevitable, one of the main things that are promise to us is death, with that say, if death waits his course, I will get to live to see my people will stop talking about problems and start solving our problems. We will realize there is no mountain steep enough that we cannot climb. We will realize there is no obstacle we cannot face and best of all we will realize there is no problem we cannot solve if we put our mind together.

Although, we have numerous challenging faces the country, due to the fact these problems have been sitting there for the past two centuries, and no sign of these problems ending in sight; is extremely discouraging to a lot Haitians. However, we have to understand we are Haitians. As poor and irrelevant we are to the world; the world fears us. The world simply fears us because of the fact of what our greatest generation did over two centuries ago. A bunch of slaves with any skilled or any trained of armed service defeated one of the greatest army that ever created by men kind. We won the battles because we believed in us; and most importantly, we acted as one. In contrast, we are now one of the most divided people in the world, and we have no confidence or even believing in ourselves. As a nation, we have to start thinking a little deeper. We have to realize the rest of the world think the worse off some part of the world is the better the other parts of the world would be. With that in mind, we have to stop hoping and wishing for the world to come and rescue us from our difficulties, in many ways, if the world was not a part of our problems, we would have been rescuing by the world. If we were hoping and wishing for the end of slave in Haiti, we would probably still be slaves, including these other slaves' nations. We must realize the fight for a better Haiti, must start with all Haitians, and ending with us all, then will realize what Haiti ought to be, one of the greatest nations of all time.

In order for us to be all that we can be, we must first start as individual ask ourselves, what can I do to better my country and in the process to better myself. As a result, the whole nation will be sound the same, we all will ask ourselves what can we do to better Haiti, and in the process to better our lives in Haiti. Then we would understand what it meant to be Haitians. You would understand it meant more than just being born Haiti to be Haitians. Being Haitians is an ideal. It is an ideal that with unity, all thing are possible. In addition, being Haitian is a witness of an advocacy for all human right of the world. Furthermore, to be Haitian is to believe every man and woman should be free and equal; which we are through the eyes of God. Most importantly, to be Haitian, is to remember 1804, wish was the day good prevailed over evil. As we understand what it meant to be Haitians, I presume we will respect and honor our country. As we were the symbol of independent for many other slave nation, we must now be the symbolize nation of prosperity, for these other entire poor nation, and if we use the same strategy we used during slavery, we will sure defeat poverty in Haiti.

As we have becoming a prosperity nation, the world would respect the Haitian people, as we deserve to be. Other nations did less for the world and have more respect in the world than us. I must say, the reasons of us not respected by the world are fair. Over 85% of the population is living well below poverty. Those Haitians people do not have the basic need to survive. We must keep in mind, those Haitians people represent our standing in the world and most importantly, they are our brother and sisters, our fathers and mothers. Water is extremely scarce in Haiti, despite surrounded by water. Those Haitian men and women do not have food to eat, even though we were feeding the entire French country during slavery. In addition, we have no healthcare system; it is dreadful to me to know in America, you cannot purchase a car, or home, without it first being insured; and yet, not a single Haitian I know that was insured when I was Haiti. If we ought to gain our respect in the world that our leaders paid for, with the same price Jesus paid for our sin; we ought to fight for these important issues. Moreover, there was a survey made in 1990, shows 85% of the population have less education than a kindergarten. If we ought to be respect by the world, we must improve that number. We must improve that number if we ought to have a seat at the world table. We must enforce all Haitian children to go to school. We should provide free school, for those whom cannot afford to go to private school. We would have free school starting from kindergarten through college, after they finish with their education, and they would have the choice waiting for them.

However, without a stable government, there will not be any solution for these problems. We are in the predicament that we are in today is because we spend the last two centuries being divided. Why the Haitians are facing these hard time someone might ask. No one really knows; but what one should know is that we should not be blaming our leaders for not sustained our unity during slavery revolution. They was not any scholar, they were slaves fighting for their dear lives. Blaming our slave leaders for the extreme division after slavery is understandable, but what is had to believe, it has been over two centuries since they freed us, and we have not made any progress yet. What is our excuse, by letting innocent children dying of hunger every day? What is our excuse, for not providing the ability to provide healthcare for ourselves especially our children? What is our excuse for not letting our senior citizens not seeing they 60th birth day. Most importantly, what is our excuse for not providing security to the Haitian people? I would like you to know, I am less interested in the blaming game, and instead, I am interested in solving the gloomy issues that we faced since two centuries ago. As a result, we must come together and solve these tremendous issues that lied in our head for over two hundreds decades. We must go back to basic, if we are going to have any chance to solve these problems. We have to understand Haiti, does not belong to any particular class of Haitians, Haiti belong to all Haitians. It does not matter if you mulattos, light skin, dark skin; it does not matter if you rich or poor, it does not matter if you over sea in other country or living in Haiti; as long as you are fighting for a better Haiti, you are more Haitians than those who are destroying Haiti. Haiti is a symbol that holds a bunch of set of ideas. Ideas such as freedom, unity, humble, harmony, love, caring, respect, love for the land of Haiti, love for the Haitian people, as long you believe in these set of values you are Haitians. Despite there are more people live in Haiti more than ever, I think we have less true Haitians right now than we did during slavery.

Indeed, since we are one nation, a better Haiti is better for us all, as we all can see, a bad haiti is bad for us all. Therefore, it is imperatives for us to unite to fight for a better Haiti. As someone who studies economics, I know if we even attempt to have a better country, we will automatically making huge improvements. I must say the journey for us to be a better country is long, but, if we start this journey together as one nation, we will endeavor a lot of ups and down, but, I am certain we will get there; we may not be able to see it, but our kids will sure see that day. The main thing we have to do is to unite as one nation to fight for a better Haiti.

CHAPTER II

Evil in Haiti

Growing up in Port-au-Prince, Haiti was extremely hard, and very intimidating. Being born December 25, 1980 in Haiti, it was like being born in Lucifer proudest little island. A little island that is an example of what Lucifer and his disciples' call home, when Jesus return to claim his people; so his people would had an idea what hell really like. But I say the bible is no longer needed to describe hell any more, I use Haiti to describe hell. If Hell is worst than living in Haiti, if I happen to go to hell after I die; I don't think God justification for putting me in hell will be justify. The evil the Haitians people do to each other is beyond human's comprehension. As early as six years old, I knew it was not normal to live the way my people chose to live their lives. When I was in preschool, it was abnormal not listening to the country most popular song prior to go to sleep. The sound of gun shots will put the country to sleep, and the sound of gun shots will wake the country up. It was a blessing to be fortunate enough to hear these song days and nights, because we know many next to us was not as lucky. Some of us were grateful for discovering our father or mother dead buddies lying down in front of our yard; To have the chance to say good bye to your love ones in Haiti was and still very rare. Not to have the peace of mind of what happen to your mother or father is not an easy thing to go through. It is extremely normal for a child to wake up and wondering when mommy or daddy is coming home. Alternatively, for a mommy and a daddy wondering what happen to their only child. Growing up in country that only brings disparity is extremely difficult. It hard in so many ways because those who really understand the problem and capable of solving the problems will never get a chance at it; but, the ones that are creating the problem are the one in charge of solving the problem, therefore make it impossible for any real solution.

By just being born in this country, nothing is promise to you. Not even the basic needs of survival, such as food, water, and shelter; the only thing that is truly promise to you is misery and death. Seeing your brother and sister burning up with tire rubber around their body up to their neck burning alive in the middle of the street, is beyond evil, and impossible to comprehend. Also, the idea someone would be broken into someone else's house at ease and taking everything, and knowing the person will get away with, was very difficult to accept. What was more challenging to accept? After those thieves took everything, the serve the victim feces to eat, and if those victims refuse to eat; they would get kill instantly. Moreover, imagine a mother and a father seeing their nine months newborn baby girl getting rape by growing man as old as forty years old. I know evils exist all over parts of the world; but the evils that are happening in this small little island are beyond the norm. These evils happened more often than a baseball player changing their white sox.

Even though I was young, I had a sense what I was seeing from my people was evil. My definition of evil at the time was something bad, twenty years later, my definition of evil still hold true. However, I knew, wherever there is evil, it is also a place amazing grace can happen. As a result, the urgency for me to grow old and try to discover the good in my people could not come any faster. The last disparity we were in, our blood set us free. This time, I have no doubt, only the good in us will set us free.

A country foundation and ideology is unity is power. Yet, this country is one of the most divide countries in the world. How have we become so disconnect to each other, when we were so united to won the slavery war against the French? Was it because of a lack of education by our liberators, or was it because we had no power and all the sudden we had too much power, and we needed more? People who do not understand the true meaning of power sees power the way vampire thirsts for blood. The more power they get, the more authority they demand. As you know demanding power could never be a good thing, but obtaining power is what true power is all about. Therefore, I think a lack of education, and lack knowledge of power is the reason why we are in this turmoil that we see ourselves in from the very beginning. The moment we go back to our foundation belief, "one for all and all for one" as it printed in our flag "l'union fait la force," The better we will restrain the survive of Haiti. In addition, if we keep going down this arrow at that pace, we all are going to be doom. As you can see, it destroyed the third class, now it is destroying the second class, and the first class will be next; and after that, there will be no class standing. Therefore, it is imperative for both classes to come together for better Haiti, because both our survival depend on it. The sooner both classes realize that, the better we will be.

I am not ashamed to acknowledge the evils in my country. To solve any problem is to know what the problem is and discuss the problem in searching of real solution. I also know every problem has a real solution, if we work together to find solutions, I project in short period of time we will see a dramatic improvement to our problem. Although, many Haitian believe there is no solution for Haiti, I deeply believe what they hoping for is a solution. As a result, just as we defeated slavery, we will defeat evil in Haiti, we will defeat poverty in Haiti, will defeat lack of education in Haiti, most important of all, we will defeat this huge division that is between us that blinding us from seeing the good in all of us. When evil die, hope will come in all over parts of Haiti. This is my promise to my unborn child, And to every Haitian in Haiti and all over the world.

CHAPTER III

Have a Vision

I have a vision. My fellow Haitians, I have come to tell you that I have a vision, one day I will be going back home. I will be going back home, not to visit, but to stay, no matter how gloomy things may be at home. I envision that all Haitians return to Haiti and reclaims Haiti back, just as the Jews have been going back to the promise land. I envision that all Haitians will for fight a better Haiti, rather than sitting down and hoping for a better Haiti. I envision that all Haitians will realize, that the wide gap between the rich and the poor; have to be reducing. I envision that our broken government one day transforms to be the model government of the world; at least for all Islanders nation. A friendly government I envision, a government that don't need to be force into the throat of other countries, but rather a model government for the world to be envy. Governments that capture the goods in all types of government such as democracy, socialism, or even communism, and reject what do not work. A friendly government as I said before. A government which believe, politician and civilians has to have mutual respect for one another, a government that break the long circle of more love for the money, but now rather more love for the country. Thus, I envision that one day our politician will love Haiti more than power and money. As we introduce new ideology for the country to live by, I would persist to insist the country must fallow. The main reason Haiti is the worse and the poorest country in the western hemisphere is because our liberators fell to introduce the ideal standard government that the country should have fallowed; instead, we were fighting among us over power. Over two centuries later, very little has change.

I envision our government will finally introduce us with new ideas that will define us as nation. As one Haitian, I believe our way of life for the country should be to put God first, then the country, then the government, last but not least family values. The greed of power and money have divided us for over two centuries, my fellow Haitians, I have come to report to you, that I envision one day those old traditions as should come to an end, rather sooner than later. I envision all Haitians reclaim our soul from the devils that we had sold on the eve of our freedom. The profit the devils have continuously making has been to steep to bear. I also envision the Haitian government has faith in the Haitian people that we are not as dumb as they believe we are; we are a nation who takes a great deal of pride in our country and our government. Therefore, wherever our government takes us, the country will follow. I envision politicians and civilians are sharing the same table; a table full of diverse and complex of ideas; ideas on how to reduce poverty in Haiti, and questioning each other on the future of our children. How is their rights is being are being protected. What are our children rights, and who protecting our children? After all, if one day this vision will become a reality, we must start with them.

As most Haitians can see, the old tradition way of living is destroying our country. Therefore, it is extremely imperatives to stop living from the past, and realize it is time to start sprinting towards the future. I envision we must not forget our past; indeed, our past is the reason for these desperate new beginning. A new beginning that should reveal what the second free nation behind the United-States in the western hemisphere should be about. Our government should invest in our children education. They also should invest in both the private and public sectors of Haiti. As an economist, I believe by investing in creating jobs, for every competent Haitians who is seeking for jobs will be beneficial for both the rich and the poor, but most importantly, it would advance the country economy as a whole. By creating jobs for every Haitians who seek to work would make Haiti relevant again; even more so, as we were during slavery to the French markets. Unlike the French, there should never be free labor in a free market. As the Haitian government is going to have the need to protect its investments, therefore the government will set up new relevant rules and regulation to protect these jobs for the Haitians citizens. I deeply believe with a roof over our head and a full stomach, we will follow any justify rules that will protect the Haitian people. I envision the government offer great deal of incentives to those in the public and the private sectors who are fighting for a better economic.

Most economists will agree with me, the only way for a government and a country to be rich and powerful is to put its to educate its people and to put its peolpe to work. I believe the biggest tools of a country economy are its people's ability to work and the country natural resources. Therefore, I envision the Haitians government invests in a variety types of resources to putting the Haitian people to work. There is no other nation more able and more willing to work than the Haitian people are at this defining moment, a moment of survival.

Even though the price of freedom is free through the eyes of God, but the price we have paid and continue to pay for our freedom is unbearable. The reward for free country is the ability for the country to make its own choices. With that in mind, how free, how we really are in Haiti? Is it our choice to choose to be the poorest country in the world? Haiti is surrounding by water. Is it our choice Haiti letting its people dying because of unclean water and hunger every day? Well above 85% of the population are unemployed, is our choice to choose not put our people to work? Also, well above 90% of the population is illiterate, is our choice not to educate our population? My vision is to envision Haitians to choose wisely. We are continuously making the wrong choices for over two centuries. As a free nation, we have earned the right to chose on to govern our country. But some how along the way, we lose our senses on how to make the right choices for our nation. What is the right choice? In simplicity, the right choice is the opposite of the wrong choice. We have to change our mind set as a nation in order for the country to realize my vision that I envision of becoming our vision one day sooner rather than later.

As you can see, my vision for Haiti is clear as the full moon. I have a vision for all Haitian all over the world to fight for a better and a safer Haiti. I vision the government invest in Haiti instead of destroying the country. By investing in protecting the country and the people of the country, would bring tourists in Haiti with their money and ready to spend in our economy. In return, they would learn about our great stories, and they would learn about our great cultures. A culture that base on great music, hope family value, pride, beauty, honesty, dignity, most importantly visionaries. I vision the government to invest in our agriculture. By investing in our agricultures, we will not have the need to import everything. By putting people to work in our farmers, the city would be less crowded, therefore there would be less trash in the city, less crime, more Haitians lives would be more productive, and as a result, our economic would be relevant to the world once again. I vision no matter what kind of class the Haitian life appear to fall in, that one thing remain vividly clear to all Haitians, that every single Haitian life matter. Also, that our future is not doom the moment of conceiving. Every Haitians has the right to decide their own destiny; we should decide on our success or failure, not for a broken government and a broken country deciding that for us.

CHAPTER IV

Something Special is About
to Happen in Haiti

I could have been your child. Now, imagine your child living in a country without any sign of hope and a peace of mind. Better yet, think of it as your beautiful innocent young child living in country without any future; but with an empty present and a gloomy past. The main problem of living in country without any hope and peace of mind, is that you get confuse. These confusions go far beyond your comprehension. As a child growing up in this hell holes call Haiti, I remember I was so confused about my place in this world, at a very early age, I started to question myself, questions such as why am I here in this world and what is my purpose in it? As I grow older, I realize I was living in a country that I believed that was not and remain unfit for children, nor for any human being for that matter. It does not shock me at all that most people who live in haiti would give their right harm to get out of it, if they could. After twenty-one years later, I acknowledge my belief remain the same. For the past two decades, there has been no change made for the better, in fact things have gotten worse far beyond any one imagination. Despite this country being one the poorest country in the world, being one of the most divided country in the world, despite this country have gotten or done anything for me, my love for this country will never flint

I love my country more than anything else does in the world. In fact, my purpose in this world is to devote my entire life to better the lives of my Haitian people. I believe a man should live his live by principles. As a result, I have three ideological principle beliefs that I am willing to die. First, I know God exist and I take it upon my faith that he gave me life and gave his life for me as I am prepare to die for him. In addition, a great philosopher says, "I believe, therefore I am". Well because of my faith, I can now say, you are; therefore, I am, because without your existence, none of us would have been possible. Even though I seem to be first, but without you, there would not be any I under any circumstances. In addition, family values are dear to my heart. I believe family is the roots of life so therefore I will die for my family values. Finally yet importantly, I am willing to die for Haiti, too many blood have shared for me to called this place home, and simply because Haiti is worth dying for. Finally, I believe, if you do not know what you are living for, then how you are going to know what to die. The ironic thing about life is that life can be prevented by abstinence, and death can't by any measure; so why put that burden of killing someone on your soul or to your conscious, when God had already say that someone should surely die. Too often, we try to do God's work instead of ours; I cannot imagine God would put us here on earth to destroying each other. Second, our greatest generation had died for our freedom. What they have done not only was great for all Haitians, but also was great for the human race. they were the first black nation to fight for human right when the white supremacy was in deep denied that we weren't human being, even though we was the same except for the color of our skin. The fact the greatest generation had the courage to die for me; I am willing to die for what has left of them, which is Haiti. Words cannot express my gratitude for their courage and the bloods they shared to give me this piece of freedom I could call my own. However, since I have faith in God, I know God is a just God, therefore I know justice will come to Haiti and to the Haitian people as soon we stop the evil seeds that have been planted upon us during slavery days. Since, we do not have any brave man left in Haiti, it is up to the cowards to call on for justice for the Haitian people; but you and I both know it is impossible to find justice in between cowards. From one brave man to another brave man and to all the cowards, the message is clear, we all needs to come together in the name of justice in order to have a better Haiti. We are one people to this beautiful land of ours; only by coming together that we have a shot to fix those difficult challenges we have faced since our existence.

Earlier, I talked about how I was living in the country without any hope and any peace of mind. The question is why a country that is responsible for millions has no hope and peace of mind for its people. As I grow older, it has occurred to me how little the Haitians people know about positives attitudes. Haiti is a country that rewards you when you do bad things and punishes when you do good things. To elaborate, François Duvalier used to punish those that was trying to go to school to better themselves, but rewards those Tonton Makout that was destroying the country. To many time we have choose evil over God, hate over love, division over unity, greed over moderation, discord over harmony, jealousy over complimentary. The older I get the more I realize the characteristics behavior are destroying Haiti, the more I realize I have to speak out. We have to change from the old ways because it is clear that it is not working. Just as negative attitude could destroy a country, Haiti is prime example; I truly believe positive attitude could repair a country as well. A country with positive attitude will do the right things for its people. A country with positives attitudes will build better school for its children, will invest in its people and put its people to work. A positive country will not except failure, but keep reaching for success. Positive country will put the country first instead of their self-interest. A positive country will produce positive leaders, as we have positive or good leaders we will have good policies. We must not giving up in this beautiful country we called Haiti, instead we must change our old ways and change for the better, we must realize Haiti's belong to all of us. Therefore, it will take all of us to fix the mess we have in our plate or the dream of seeing better Haiti will seem far less possible.

If we work hard, we may not get to see the beauty that we all know Haiti could be; but I promise you our grand children will get to see it. The Haitian people are hungry for a little hope, we just would like to see a leader come along and give us that thirst we have been so desire. I am being very optimistic that this leader will come with the right message for us. We can only hope fear does not delay the inevitable. From one Haitian, to another, let me be the first one to break the news to you, something special is about to happen in Haiti, I can only hope, I live long enough to get to see it.

CHAPTER V

The Reasons Why Haiti is the Poorest Country in the Western Hemisphere

As we all know, Haiti is the poorest country in the western hemisphere and one of the poorest country in the world. Its per capita income is about less than $400, this considerable far worst than the rest of the world. As for the United States, its per capita is over $33,000, unarguably one of the best in the world. Sadly, to say well above 90 percent of the rural Haitian population live below poverty. Rather for us to see improvement, things have gotten worst instead. For example, for the past two decades employee rate have decline in per capita by 5.2 percent between the years of 1985-1995, and from the year of 1995-2005 the employee rate have decline in per capita at a rate of 15.5 percent. With that in mind, we have to be optimistic about our future. There will be a time that we will stop moving backward, but moving toward a brighter future. This day will a new beginning.

As we searching for solution to solve our country economics problems, we have to understand what causes the problems. First, the question we must all raise as citizens of this great nation, why we are so poor. A question Haitian must ask themselves and I believe have raised many time before, but not every one of us understands the magnitude of relevancy to this question. Only the answer to this question will solve the problems to our economic . . . Why Haiti is the poorest country in the western hemisphere? To answer this question, I have to break it down in three series. First o all, the international community play a big role to this tiny black nation on the reason why we so poor. All of it started with the French nation. The French nation really put the famous phrase by Julius Caesar, I came, and I saw, I conquer to work, when it had came to Haiti. They came to this tiny island and went to West Africa and conquered the people of that nation to be their slaves; Depriving them of their lands, their religion, their values and worst of their entire God given right as human being. The French nation shipped these innocent black men and women to this tiny island called Haiti. There, they worked endlessly for the French nation under the worst condition humanly possible. Because of their hard work, in the mid of 1750, economists estimate that Haiti provide as much as 50% of the Gross National Product of France. The French nation used to import coffee, sugar, cotton, cocoa, tobacco, finally yet importantly dye indigo. These incredible men and women make the French nation the most powerful nation in the world. What were they in returned? More deprivation of their rights as human being, they were not allowing of an education. They were not allow to love one and other, they were not allow to practice their belief, they were not allow to practice family values, the only thing they were allowed to do is to worked endlessly for the rest of their lives. The French nation govern the tiny island the opposite way the British govern the united states; as a result, the united stated is the best and most powerful country in the world, and Haiti is the poorest country in the world.

Also, because the international boycott of Haiti to have the right of its independency from the French nation, result into the biggest blonder of Haiti politic history ever. A country that was holding by a threshold economically and politically, pay the French nation a large sum amount of money to recognize them as a nation; the lack of education during slavery really paid for the French nation; soon after this huge payment. The country collapsed economically and politically kept downward at a speed of lights and things would never get better. The principle the French nation implement during slavery to our people is the reason why we are the poorest country in the western hemisphere if not the world.

The invasion of the United States to Haiti is also one of the reasons why Haiti is one of the poorest countries in the world. I would like to state the obvious and what millions would be to afraid to say. Let us go back in time to the 1900s; American was a country control by whites who thought black people was inferior at the time. In facts, they treat the black that was in their country worse than their pets. With that in mind, I find it extremely difficult that they would could come to Black Country and help them for the better when they could not help their kind in their own country. I believe Haiti is still weeping from this occupation from the United States.

Until there is clarity from the United States policy to the Haitians, Haiti will continue to be a fail states.

The next series of the reason why Haiti is so poor, I believe is the lack of accountability of the Haitians lawmakers. Corruption should not be tolerate, but expected it has come to politicians. However, the Haitians governments let corruption dominate the politic system of Haiti. At the early ages, one can conclude that was expected. Thanks to the French, We were a young nation that was ignorance and illiterate. For that reason, we were doomed to fail. There is a reason even to this day almost 90% of the population remain illiterate. Any country white or black have that majority of its people are illiterate is doom to fail. Now, it has been over two centuries since we have been free; when are we going to adopt and act as a free nation. I know a numerous of factors are responsible for us being one of the poorest country in the world, but, the main reason we remain poor is us, the Haitians people.

To elaborate, we have a system of education that is failing our kids. We speak Creole at home and school, but the teacher teaches us in French; as if I used to understand those subjects those teachers used to teaching me. We study a bunch of subject, which is so irrelevant to our culture and our way of life. Rather for you to teach us life skills lessons that would help us to build a better country, rather you teaching us Latin, Spanish, English, French, like these are really going to put food in our table.

Last but not least, the lack of investment in the Haitians people. the French nation give us the blue point on how to have a successful economy, yet we cherry picked all the terrible things they implanted to our brain and rejected the most important lesson of all that Haiti is an agriculture country. We do not have to practice their ideological way of doing business, but we could used the lesson of hard work equal rewards.

I know it possible that Haiti could be a major player in the world economy, because we have done it before. Historian say, Haiti, once called the jewel of the Antilles, and was the richest colony in the entire world. During slavery, Haiti provides as much as 50% of the Gross national product of entire France. They way they have done was simple, they put people to work. We do not have to slave our people, but, if we put people to work, I promise in matter of decade Haiti would be a force in the world economy just as we were during slavery. If we focused in the same thing the French use to focused on, such as coffee, cocoa, cotton tobacco, dye indigo and cotton, rice, ect . . . as an economist, we will be the country that stop begging for help and be the country that helping those that are begging. I hope that be a model for those countries to stop begging, just as were the model countries that end slavery.

Finally, the last series but not least of the reason why Haiti is one of the poorest countries in the world; First, I would say the lack of justice are the biggest puzzle link to the level of poverty in Haiti. Some of us might reject to believe that the average Haitians life expectancy is only 55 years old compare to the United States the average life of expectancy is 73. There are many reasons for this huge gap, but the main reason is education percentage between the two countries. Expert say over 85% of the Haitians population is illiterate. Less than 20% of the population has rich secondary school. There is no relevant health care system establishment in Haiti. Most of the population is living in condition that is not humane. However, in spite of all of that, our population continues to grow at a high rate estimated at 200, 1000 or more per year. As you can see, this factor is doom to fell the country, high population growth, lack of investment of social infrastructure, inadequate roads, inadequate energy system, water system, sewage, inadequate health care system, worse of all inadequate education system.

Haiti, would not be fix over night, but, with a little bit of hope, and if confronted these problems, I have know doubt, in a matter of decade, we will make great progress, progress far beyond we thought was once possible.

CHAPTER VI

If I was the President

If I had the honor to be the president of this great, country of Haiti, regardless of where you are in the world, my number one job would be to protect Haiti and the Haitian people by any mean necessary. Despite of being rich or poor, children or seniors citizens, gay or straight, Christian or atheists, literate or illiterate, they all would be protect under the sky of the Haitian land by the same merit, innocent until proven guilty. To illustrate, to have a fair and balance country, all Haitian citizen must be equal under the court of law, until proven guilty otherwise. After all, in God view, all men and women are equal, so therefore, equality would be necessary if I was the president of Haiti. If I were the president of Haiti for instant, the law would not be blind through the eyes of the rich, and be in plain sight when it comes to the poor. The rewards and the punishments would be equal as for the rich and the poor. Despite the fight I would anticipate from the rich or the poor, mostly from the rich for fighting for a better Haiti; I know it would be almost impossible to defeat. As you and I both know, when the establishment is well establishing changes is hard to come. For example, despite how poor the country of Haiti is, which is one of the poorest country in the world; I believe, every Haitians know Haiti is one the best country to live in, if you fortunate enough to have money. In fact, if you do a survey by asking every Haitians in this world, is Haiti is one the best country to live in, when you have money? I guarantee you the high positive result would be a shocking to you. Most Haitians, if not all Haitians believed Haiti is one the best country to live in, when you have wealth. As a result, fighting the wealthy Haitians to fight for a better Haiti would be like fighting the Roman Empire army. Despite how gloomy the situations is for the common

Haitians, it doesn't' bother the rich, because they exclude themselves as being one of us, forgetting the common bond we all have, the first black nation to fight for human equality and won. However, I have come to remind them, the common person will rise again. If the common man and woman could defeat slavery, I have no doubt in my mind; the common man and woman will defeat poverty in Haiti. In fact, I am willing to bet my life and my soul on it. After all, I must say, if embarking these issues was not challenging in the first place, I am convince they would be tackled already. As a result, if I were the president of Haiti, embarking upon these challenging issues would be my priority one, no matter how difficult and gloomy these challenges may happen to be. I believe poverty can only be defeated in Haiti by our ancestor ideology unity is power. With that in mind, I know through out my life, It's clear to me that nothing is impossible when we are unify in fighting for a common cause that are greater than ourselves, and what greater than ourselves to fight to better your country.

If I were the president Haiti, no Haitians children would be over looked down on. As your president, we would not be forgetting our past, indeed our past is the reason for these desperate new beginning. As a young Haitian child and I could speak for many other, that we were ignored growing up. We ignored by our parents, and worse of all we were ignored by our government. Our government main purpose is to provide securities for those whom cannot protect themselves, and yet as a young child in Haiti, I was ignored. In facts, I felt like I did not exist through out my teenage years. My own father was abusing me; and no one came to my rescue. I could have been beaten by the T.V. code extension, night and days, no authorities would come to my rescued, I would not even get a knocked at my door, as for in effort to stop these bleeding from my beloved father. Even though, I could hear my mother tears through the door on the other side of the room; there is nothing she could have done for me; like my father would say, "she is nothing, she was not even good enough him. "The biggest mistake I made in my life is marrying that idiot." However, little did she know, these tears hurt more than these beating I was getting from my father. Little did she also know; those same tears would stop me from committed suicide every time I anticipated too which was many. In addition, my family could be at sleep in he middle of the night, and buglers would broke into my house and take every thing we own, and there is no authorities to call, no investigation would be engage, even though sometime we have been beating and slapped around, there would be no justice for my family. The Haitians people and the Haitians children have been looking down for far too long; I have no doubt in my mind, If was the president of Haiti, my priority one, would be to protect every Haitians; especially those Haitians who cannot protect themselves. That what leaders do, that is what I would be doing if I were the president of Haiti, even if I would have to give up my life.

As president, I would be moving to a new positive attitude with a new direction we all would agree on, moving away from our horrible past and these hopeless present times, and move toward a crystal future. For the first time in our life, we would be focus toward a brighter future, a brighter future that would start with our children. We would start by educating every single Haitian child in Haiti. We would send our teacher to study abroad and come back to teach our kids. We would build competent public school all over Haiti, from grade kindergarten to universities. Instead of countries send us money, we would ask them to give us books, computers, and the knowledge they possess in other for us to be truly independent. Haiti is known as the poorest country in the world, if was the president of Haiti, Haiti would known as the country that protect and educate their children. As a result, two centuries later, I would have no doubt in my mind; Haiti would have been the richest and one of the best countries in the world. Because of my strong belief in education, if I was the president of Haiti, I would make sure I invest every single resources Haiti has left to the children of this great nation. Therefore, we would have been the smartest, and the brightest children in the world. If I were the president, I would be the first to tell you these tasks would extremely be challenging, if not impossible, but, if I were the president, I would also be the first one to tell you, if any nation can do it, it would definitely be the Haitians people. If I was, I was the president of Haiti; children would have rights; and every Haitians citizen would know these rights. There would be many strong programs all over parts of the country, to help every Haitians Child that is in need. These programs would be their voice, when they would cry to speak from the evils that confronted them. In addition, no Haitian children would be uneducated; it would be these program duties to make sure every Haitian child are educated until the age of eighteen and beyond. If I were the president of Haiti, education would not be a privilege of our children; education would be a right to all Haitians children. To exemplify, one the saddest thing of my life, is every time my mother have to sign her named, she become blind, she would literally tell me she can't see; she would write a cross, or I would shyly write her name on the doted line. The biggest problem we face in our country since slavery; is that each generation from the past do very little to educated and protect the children of this great nation, so as a result, we have been headed to the same downward direction generation, after generation; as president. I would have done everything in my power to change that long-standing tradition. First thing I would do, If was the president of Haiti, I would wake up everyday and fight for our children protection and their education; they are the roots of our country and they have been ignored for far too long; as president, they would have been my priority one.

If I were the president of Haiti, our senior citizens would not be forgotten. As you ages in Haiti, they seem to look down on our senior citizens. If I were the president of Haiti, instead of looking down on our senior citizen, we would be looking up to them. I would encourage the population to learn from our senior citizen mistake and their weaknesses. Every Haitians life is extremely important, so as your president, I would do anything to preserve every Haitians lives; especially our young children and our senior citizens because of the fragility of their life. If was the president of Haiti; I would invest in senior citizen programs in order for them to live a complete life. I would invest in health care, by creating a great deal of hospital and clinic as I can. In addition, as your president, I would build as many universities as I can all over part of the country. I would invest in doctors, and would give them great incentive such as free education for a certain numbers years in return for their services. I would invest in our scientist, so they could invest in research for medicine to better our senior citizens lives. If I was the president of Haiti, not only our senior citizen would not be for gotten, if I was the president of Haiti, for the very first time, the light would be as bright as the morning sun on the Haitians people. If I was the president of Haiti, my honesty and loyalty would be in front and center to the Haitian people; I strong believe, the only way to rescue Haiti from these two gloomy times, is to engage an a common trust from the leaders of Haiti and the Haitians people. I know the Haitian people lose faith and do not trust their government and their government system. Fairly to say we should. However, we should not be sole blame the government for our entire problems; we should bare some the responsibilities for our problems, otherwise, things will never change for the better. We must keep in mind; the governments are made off our children, so, the characters, the attitudes and the values we raised them up with as family, and will the same principal values they will govern us with. So, we must understand we have to do our parts as Haitians citizens, to be accountable first by doing the right thing for our children, so when their grow up, they grow up to be great citizens; and most importantly great leaders.

If I was the president, these are the messages I would encourage us to put into practice, only a strong and positive message that could lead us out to the predicament that we are in. If I were the president of Haiti, trusting the Haitian people to fight for a better Haiti would have been my priority one in office. As the Haitians people are getting wiser, they would understand, I would not be able to do it all alone; as a result, I believe all Haitian would be participating in the of fight to better Haiti.

Next, if I were the president of Haiti, I would expand the police force. I would create new level of policies such as "federal bureau of investigation" known as FBI in the United States of America. I think that is a very important program in the U.S.A, as president of Haiti I would adapt this program. The best thing about this program, it would protect the Haitian people and would create jobs at the same time for the people.

In addition, I believe the most important thing of my presidency would the balance of power; as the people give me the power to the presidency, I would turn a round and give the power back to the people, as it should be. I would create a new permanent law, which would be calling *L'union fait la force*. This law would enable the people to vote for a judge that was born and raise in their state and each one of these judges would be the voice of the people to the white house, instead of having one people fighting for them as the president. Now they would have a variety of people fighting for them for a better Haiti. If I were the president of Haiti, giving power back to the people would be my priority one. These judges combine would have great power and can challenge the president, if the president is not fighting on the behalf of the Haitian people, with an unanimous request of the people, these judges can impeach the president if violating the law and betray the Haitian people. For example, the concept is no one person is greater, the than the Haitian people voice, not even the sitting president. So therefore, the country would go whichever direction the Haitians people would be willing to take it. Indeed, both the president and these judges would have to make decision in the best interest of all the Haitians people. The agenda of the Haitian citizens would finally be in the equal ground. In simplicity of this law, it has to carry out the Haitians people voice, when the Haitians people asking to speak as a whole to the white house. These judges would have no term, they will be judge for the states for life unless breaking the law of the land and the president would have the right to appoint the best judge from that states with the improvement with majority of the people of that state. If I was the president of Haiti, Haitians people would finally have a voice at the table; a voice their fought to have since slavery; and over two centuries later they yet too seem to be head no matter how loud they are screaming, as president of Haiti, their voice would have been finally be head al over the world.

Last, but not least, if I was the president of Haiti, jobs creation both in the private and public sectors would be my priority one. As a result, I would invest all my sweat and blood in the Haitian people. The reason being is that, I strongly believe the number one tool of the Haitians population, is the Haitians people. In fact, I fundamentally believe the number one tool of any nation, is its people. To illustrate, America, is one of the best country in the world; and Haiti, is one of the worst country in the world. As a result, every Haitians would like to leave Haiti, and come to live in America; thinking this is their solution to their problem. However, I would suggest to both the Americans and the Haitians to an empirical event. Although this experience would be impossible to accomplish, theatrically speaking, if the Americans and the Haitians people trading countries, and both population remain with their core values; I wouldn't have no doubt in my mind, as the American live in Haiti, Haiti would now have been one of the best country in the world and Haitians now live in America, America would have now been one of the worst countries in the world. Indeed, every Haitians would now leave America and come to Haiti, in searching of a better life. Some critics would say that is not a good comparison to compare Haiti and America, and those critics would total be missing the whole point of my argument. The argument I am making comparing these two countries together is not about the size of each country, it is an argument about the system of each country implement in each country. I believe countries like America understand the power of choice, and countries like Haiti do not understand the power of choice. From being rising in both countries, I conclude a real theory about choices. I have realized that choices have only two outcomes, no matter how many choices you have in front of you. You could have a trillion of choices; the outcome could be either good or bad. In addition, all the stuff in between, is there to distract you from one of the real choices which either is bad or good; or yes or no; or God or evil, male or female ect . . .

The sooner the third world countries adapt my theory, the sooner they will serve their people with the right choice. The choice of engaging or choice not to engage; if I was the president of Haiti, the choice would be very clear to me I would choose to engage the Haitians people, in our quest of fighting for a better Haiti.

I deeply believe it does not matter how poor a country is, if the country engage to be rich, it would be rich. I am a strong believer in the word of God; the word say if you knock at the door, the door shall be open. As a result, as president of Haiti, I would not stop knocking at that door. My first knock would be to restore confidence to the Haitians people, I would have made them realize, what it is truly mean to be Haitians. The Haitians is nations that believe nothing is impossible. The idea that the Haitians people cannot defeat poverty in Haiti is the most outrages myth that ever existed in the world. In addition, the idea the Haitians people cannot be united to fight for a better Haiti is also a myth. I believe Haitian can fight for peace, Haitian can fight for jobs, Haitian can fight for security, Haitians can fight for better care of every Haitians, Haitians can fight for family value, the Idea that we cannot is the biggest barrier between us. However, I ought to remind us, if we can defeat slavery and defeat the napoleon army as slave I found hard to believe that we cannot fight our own demons.

However, because of the world law was created by rich country, these laws protect the rich to be richer and the poorer is to be poorer, we must understand as one of the poorest country in the world. We have to understand fighting to better our country is not going to be a pleasant pill to swallow by these rich countries. As a result, they are going to send a bunch of curve balls out our way; to discourage us; we should well these curve balls. The more curve balls they send at us the closer we will be to our goals. These will be the sings of never to give up. In addition, I will be the first one to tell you, this revolution will be harder than the one we fight during slavery; and because the enemy is among ourselves, the sacrifice that we would have to make, would be greater than what we made during slavery. Some of us are our own enemies; we will not be able to fight for a better Haiti, until all of us are in the same page as a country. Every Haitians are in title of their freedom, but your freedom must not conflict another Haitian freedom. As a result, with that new fundamental belief, every Haitians has the right to be protected under sky of the beautiful land; it should not be matter what you Ideological belief are; because we are a free nation, we are in title of difference of opinion. However, what no friend is entitled are to take our freedom from us without justification. Haiti has become Haiti, because slavery was not justified; and somewhere along the way, we fail to acknowledge what it truly means to be Haitians. I believe all of us should be in the same fight as we are in the same boat, a fight to protect every living being in Haiti. As people of Haiti, we would invest in the security of our land. In addition, we would invest in education, especially the next generation; finally yet importantly, we should invest in our farmers. If we ought to get out of this struggle time, we must go back to our worse day and go back to Haiti best days. Haiti best days was when Haiti was the leading export of the world mainly trough out Europe. I know because of erosion that will be hard for Haiti to go back to its golden days. But, I know with a little change of behavior towards the environment, a little investment in technology, most importantly create the tools and protect to tools our farmers need survive; I have no doubt we can be relevant in the world economy again.

If I was the president, no Haitian in this world should be struggle for basic need of survival. For a long time it has been an automatic choice for our people to live without the basic things you need to survive. There are many reason for that; one of the main reason in particular, I believe it is extremely hard for a family to stand firm on their own two feet, when the head of the household isn't being productive in providing for the family. So is not that hypocritical to believe Haiti will remain standing when the head of the country is not being productive. Indeed, someone who is constantly asking for a hand out and is not making any effort to better him or her will gain no respect from you. I believe the same would say for countries. To illustrate, what was once a huge player in the world economy, now, have become so irrelevant to the world. The world would not miss it a bit if ought to depart away from the world. Therefore, therefore the world does not care too much of our existence. As a result, as our doom day looming up on us like the speed of light not one soul coming to our rescue even the main one that partly responsible for our misery.

One will never know the true reason why we have falling so far away from the modern world. However, in my view, I believe this is beyond Haiti and the Haitian people. One thing I know for certain, that Haiti has been in punishment by the supreme by being an advocate for freedom, which I find very ironic. The way they cherish freedom, you would think Haiti would have been their best allies. The fact remain we are not a descendent of the supreme of the world, so therefore we had no right to fight for freedom at the time we did. If there is a point that needed to be me made, I must say point well made. However, as Haitian people, the poverty war that falling up on our head is a war we cannot afford to lose. Although poverty been leading us for a long time, but, if we get defeated by pervert we may as well kiss good-bye to our existence. Poverty has the biggest weapon in the world. Poverty weapons are lack of education, lack of water and food, and poverty biggest weapon is crime; if not all of us are stand up to this war in poverty, we all are going to be doom and gloom in a very short period. If I was the president of Haiti, the poverty war is a war I would make every Haitian be aware of, educate, and make them realize this is bigger than the one we defeated a little over two centuries ago.

CHAPTER VII

Toussaint

One man dream died in Paris, as a result, a whole nation dream in Haiti.
Haiti's country of dream, but when the dream will begins.
Blame the French for all Haitians misfortunes.

Haiti liberated since 1804, but far from being a free

Yes indeed, we were liberating from the France since 1804; but we were far being free from the negatives lessons we had endured from the French during slavery. The lack of education during slavery has to do with the key problems we are now facing today in Haiti two centuries later. For example, even after over two centuries after liberating from the French, over 85 percent of the population is uneducated. More over, Haiti is one of the poorest countries in the western hemisphere; perhaps the world, simply because of the lack of investment the French did during slavery. As we all know, Haiti had an abundance of the world best resources during slavery, but, when the French was ruling Haiti, they only had one mission in mind; the mission was to take everything in Haiti and expedited it to French. A mission that was so critical to the way of life of the French, as you can imagine, letting go of these life styles was not an option the French could have fathomed at the time. In fact, the demand for these life styles spread through out the whole continent of Europe. As a result, for these high demands of that life style, the French had to create new ways to met theses higher demand of the French people. As a result, the French went to Africa, they take us from our roots, divided us from our unity and loving culture for one another; in return we get to spend our entire life in misery. Indeed, the system the

French implemented or the foundation of Haiti was extremely inhumane, so therefore, I believe the reason why the majority of Haitian population is profoundly living so inhumanely conditions was because of the lack of interest the French had, not only to the Haitians, but also the lack of interest the French had Haiti to stand alone.

The French may have a valid argument not to bear any responsibilities for the ongoing political chaos in Haiti since the French left Haiti a little over two centuries ago. After all, it has been too long since the French left Haiti, to bear any responsibilities for the Haitians own misfortune. In my view, this argument would be a valid argument to make and a very strong argument to make. Time after time, since the French left, the Haitians have done nothing to progress their own country they have insanely died for to call their own. Rather, first thing they did, was to divide the country into two countries. The next thing they did, was assassinated the very first leader of the country who goes by Jean-Jacques Dessaline. This pattern started a short period after the French left Haiti, and this pattern has been an ongoing pattern two centuries later after the French left. The lack of governments' stability started with the existence of Haiti, and which I believe are the sources of which that are crippling the existence of Haiti at this present time.

The hypocrisy of the French nation began unarguably with the best leader Haiti ever had. In fact, the best leader the world had ever seen before, the leader that defeated the great Napoleon. A great man that goes by the name of Toussaint L'Ourverture, Toussaint Louverture, was born may 20, 1743. He was born in Cape de Haiti; he was a strong believer in catholic. He was a self-educated man. He was the architect of the Haitian successful revolutionary battle against the French, the British, and the Spanish during slavery. During his short governor life, between 1800 and 1802, Toussaint Louverture tried to rebuild the collapsed economy of Haiti and reestablish commercial contact with the United States and Great Britain. As brilliant as Toussaint Louverture was, he still failed for the false friendship the French offered him as an equal partner with the French. As a result, Toussaint Louverture died in exile in France in April 8, 1803. He was only 59 nine years old. His last message was to the France, "you may cut the tree, but, the roots of the tree go beyond the tree." In addition, his last words to his son were, "my boy, you will one day go back to Haiti; forget that France murdered your father".

Now as I look at the state of Haiti, how can I forget the hypocrisy of the France toward Haiti? Would Haiti still be a fail state or still remain irrelevant to the world if the France did not killed our gifted leader prior to his prime.

Now, the country Toussaint Lourverture died for cannot protect its own people, financially, socially, or even militarily. As I look back at Toussaint great legacy, it gives me great hope that Haiti will become a great country, just as Toussaint vision it to be.

I cannot envision that was the vision Toussaint had in mind, when he was fighting to abolish slave in Haiti. I vision Toussaint vision, one day that the France will recognize Haiti as independent states, which is well capable of being standing alone. I vision Toussaint vision, to work together with the French as equal partner in all aspect possible, financially, socially, economically, even military. I vision Toussaint vision mutual respect from the French, has Haiti been transitioning from being a slave state. I vision Toussaint vision seeking mentor from the French while working on developing Haiti. As one man dream died in Paris, as a result, an entire nation dream died in Haiti.

Haiti is a country of dream, simply, because the Haitians people have a numerous amounts of hope and dream. However, when will the dream begin? As Haitians citizens, even though you do everything that Haiti has asked of you, yet, Haiti has done nothing you ask of it. To illustrate, you may go to school, received a great education, being a great citizens, you would still not get a job after you have finished with your education. What more absurd about Haiti, is the huge gap between the rich and the poor. Well above 90% of the population is living below extreme poverty. There are a lack of effort in Haiti by the lawmakers to propose and enforce law and regulation to bridge the gap between the rich and the poor. In addition, there is a lack of effort to better the Haitians lives in Haiti, for example, the lack of effort for great domestic policies in Haiti, is a huge misfortune by the Haitian lawmakers in Haiti. Healthcares, education, energy, Tax, economic, highway patrol, all are misfortune policies the Haitians governments fail to reform. I believe the Haitian governments are failing to reform the policies I mention above, not because they do not like Haiti or they do not have any interest in the Haitians people. Our governments simply do not have the knowledge on how to reform these policies. The French failed to educate the Haitians during slavery, with the level of education the French has on these policies, I believe its not only the Haitians obligation to seek for knowledge on these keys policies, but, it is also the French obligation to help educate the Haitians, if the Haitians wisely enough to ask of it.

Moreover, the corruptions between the governments, which started with the existence of Haiti, make it impossible for any resolution. Although, Haiti is a democratic country, our voice is far from being head. It is as we in mute controlled, we have screamed, yelled, shouted to our government about the direction Haiti is going, and nothing has change. In fact, Haiti has gotten worse in the past two decades. The Haitian governments have failed the Haitians people since their existence. Although not the government entire fault, one should wonder, when is enough is enough?

Enough will be enough when the Haitians government approaches things in a different direction. The slaves' mentality they have endured during slavery is what destroying Haiti and treating Haiti own existence as of this present time. As Haiti facing their gloomiest moment beside slavery in history, I believe the Haitians need to come together, and open their eyes, to confront these critical issues head on for any chance of a better Haiti. I know in dark time times, it is easy to close your eyes, rather to let them open, but if we as Haitian think, the solutions for Haiti are going to be easy, our eyes might remain closing forever.

For all the misery, the French put the Haitians through, it is extremely hypocritical of the French, not helping the Haitians to educate themselves on how o better Haiti. The world knows the condition of Haiti is close to disaster, and yet the world has closed their eyes to the Haitians people, as if they are not a part of this world. There are millions of people are living inhumanely in Haiti. It breaks my heart seeing young Haitians kids eating dirt for breakfast, dinner and supper every day for their survival. Despite that, many of them are dying of hunger every day. Those children is not guilty of anything, except for being born in Haiti, as a result, they have met their death sentences much sooner any of them had anticipated.

As I mention earlier, more than 90% of the population is illiterate, and well above 90% of the population is living well below poverty. It is a vicious time that started with the French during the slaves' era, and it is something that is continue to the Haitians and it is something the Haitians have yet to have under control. If history showed us anything about our misfortune, it shows us we have to fix our own misfortunes, although it would be helpful if other countries help. Another word, if we were sitting on the sideline as we are today, we would have never have been liberated from the French. We the Haitians must not wait any longer for the world to come to our rescue. I have seen this moment in time as critical moment for the Haitians generation, and we should approach as such. We should break from ourselves, we have tight rope we have been hanging around our neck since slavery, and this rope time is more than over due. I believe it is time for a new revolution, a revolution from us. We have been our own worse enemy about successful in Haiti. In fact, we have been destroying Haiti ever since our independence day. Those many unworthy dictatorship, those fake presidents, for the past two centuries have contributed on the destruction of Haiti and the Haitians people. If our grand parents were educated during slavery, our parents would have been educated as free men, then we would been educated as free country, then Haiti, would not have so many illiterate people, and therefore, Haiti would not have so many unworthy leaders. Although, our misfortune is not the entire French fault; but, it is unarguable that our misery started with the French.

CHAPTER VIII

The Economic Solution For Haiti

The complexity of the Haitian economy will need government intervention. Therefore, the solutions for these problems will not be simple due to the lack proficient of the Haitians government and the lack of trust the Haitian public has toward their leaders. Nevertheless, the government should focus on solving the economic problems of the Haitian economy. Most economists would agree with me, no country in the world could sustain a downward economic for long period and sustain it existence. There are many way the Haitian government can chose to solve the economic problems in Haiti, however, as an economist point of view, first I think the Haitian government should start secure and strengthen the government assets. Next, the government of the Haitian would need to focus on the macroeconomic stability while setting policies to encourage both the public and private sectors of their survival. Finally yet importantly, the government should focus on educating the people while raising the level per capital in Haiti.

Our government has to deal with a huge economic chaos. First thing the government need to do, is to strengthen any institution that own by the government, while gaining and maintain political stability. Since we do know how incapable the Haitian government is, therefore the Haitian people would have to get assistant from the intentional world with the condition of being the head of the bunch. Anyhow, because of the limited resources of our country, first it is imperial for the government to maintain its role to the areas that are fragile. The government should understand it cost money to govern, so therefore, the government will need to secure any source of income coming to the government. In addition, the government needs to create new methods of new source of income. Those income must not be going to fraud politician, instead the government should deposit these capital to a government branch known has treasury in the United States for the development of the country. One of the main things our government will need to do is to create jobs. As the government created jobs, and protect and give great incentives to the private sectors, the government will also create new source of income. Some of the most profitable source of incomes for any country are the taxes, therefore, the government will need to refocus on it tax laws, and make sure it work for the country.

Next, the government will also need to secure property rights, and create new regulator for both the public and the private sector in the country. As the government has more capital, the government should invest in infrastructure; next, the government will need to design a structure to deal with the health and education issues especially in t the crowded areas. The country will be going to numerous changes, therefore, the executive and the parliament branch of government will need to work entirely together in order for the country to succeed. In addition, the leaders of the Haitian people should tear down the centralized organizational structure of the government, and rebuild it as a decentralize organization. This would require the leaders to have trust among the government official. Decision would no longer be made in centralize place. The local elected officials should make decision for their local area with regard of the executive leader; and best of all, decision should be base in the best interest of the public. Next, Strengthen macroeconomic stability and reduce distortions in order to encourage private sector investment and increase productivity. Boosting private investment will provide the underpinnings of Haiti's future economic growth. An important first step will be implementing the Capitalization program, in particular the telecommunications, electricity, water sector, ports and airports. Privatization of these sectors will increase the productivity of the economy and demonstrate the government's commitment to redefine the role of the state and set the economy on a modern course. The government has made significant efforts to maintain macroeconomic stability, which needs to be continued and strengthened. advance the quality of government spending, invest in the provision of basic human needs, and raise the level of human capital. A huge challenge for the Haitian government will be increasing resources allocated to financing social services. In education, health, water and sanitation, and family planning, the government should continue to leave the delivery of these services to the private sector with government supervision, while government strives to improve the regulatory framework and coordinates its own activities, those of private actors, and the rich and the poor themselves should trust the government are working for them. Limited government resources should be directed at programs targeted to the very poor, particularly those in rural areas that have been neglected in the past. Until the benefits of these longer-term investments in human capital are felt, the existence of targeted transfers and social safety net programs will continue to be important to the survival of the Haitian population.

Last but not least, external givers are important to the Haitian people yet crucial to their survival in the recovering in the long term. This cause two main serious problem I believe for the Haitian people when over seas flood the country with money without any type of productivity by the Haitian people. First, it made the Haitian people lazy, to go look for job or creating job for their own survivor. These Haitians are extremely unproductive as a result make the country at a standing still while the result of the world is moving forward at a fast rate. That would not be so painful if the government was making up for production by taxing these donors, and invest in infrastructure, education, hospitals, last but, not least, agriculture.

CHAPTER IX

Haiti Country of Dream

Every Haitian knows without a doubt that Haiti is a country of dreams. The question that need to be raise by the Haitian people, what is that dream? Many Haitian who live in Haiti know what that dream is. It is a dream that every Haitians in the world hope for a better Haiti in the future. Indeed, The question in every Haitian mind, when will the dream begin? It is factual to say the Haitian people has been dreaming of a better Haiti since our existence, two centuries later, our dream of a better Haiti is getting deeper into in endless nightmare. There are many reason for this nightmare; however, the main reason for this nightmare are, each generation that passes through Haiti, have hope for a better Haiti, as they are hoping for a better Haiti, they have done absolutely nothing to bring this dream into reality. Worse of all, they believe the next generation, will bring the much needed changes that the Haitians needs and deserve while in the mean time embark the country into a deeper nightmare. However, when the next generation arrived, the next generation adopted the same failed mentality as the previous generation. This gloomy cycle has doomed the Haitian population for centuries. The question, that need to be raise, what generation that will actually begin the most difficult tasks for Haiti since slavery, perhaps even bigger than slavery.

As one of the proudest Haitian, it is extremely important, for my generation to reject, the old ways of doing business as usual. What if the Toussaint Louverture generation only hoped for freedom instead of fighting for freedom, where would we be as a country? We probably would still be lock down in chain being slaves. We probably would still digging our own holes in the ground, burry our buddy except for our face and let our French master pouring syrups on our face for ants and rats to come devoured us alive. We probably still are separate from our babies' right after birth to be raised as slaves. We would probably still be being whipped as Jesus did before his death. We probably remain unworthy as a human being. We have to understand while hoping is great; progressive toward hope is even greater. When we stand up and begin to fight all the issues that are treating our civilize existence in this world, this moment in time will be the greatest moment of Haiti since the abolishment of slavery.

Sometimes, I wonder what makes Haitians people proud to be Haitians. We are the poorest country in the western hemisphere according to World Bank. We have a political system that is extremely unstable, our literacy is the worse in the western hemisphere; our GDP is one of the worse in the world. Our life expectancy is the shortest according to World Bank. Then, why is that we remain one of proudest country in the world? As a proud Haitian myself, I did not have to rock my brain to know the only things that makes us proud, it is the same thing that is shaming us. The only proud moment of Haiti history is the abolition of slavery as the first black nation to do so. Shameless to say, over two centuries later, we yet to find anything else to make us proud, it is clear, we were not ready to be independent, although we were clear ready to be free from slavery.

How do we end this endless nightmare? First thing we need to do is to unit under our flag. We have to understand for which that flag stand up for, which is life, liberty, and the pursuit of happiness. What are life, liberty and happiness? According to Webster dictionary, life is the condition that distinguishes organism from inorganic objects and dead organism, reproduction, being manifest by growth to metabolism, reproduction, and the power of adaptation to environment through changes originating internally. Knowing the definition of life, make me wonder is Haiti alive as a country. One may raise this question, what makes a country alive? First, a country is alive, when it providing security for its entire people. It should not matter if you are rich or poor, living in the city or a slum village, it should not matter of what your status is, and the entire people in the country should obey the law. Any one that fails to obey the law by any circumstances should be present to legitimate judge and be prosecuting if he or she is guilty. A country is alive when the country is protecting the interest of it entire people. World development statistics show Haiti and many other countries like Haiti, are some the poorest country in the world, because too often, individual put their interest first instead of the interest of the entire people in the country. Economist would be an agreement with me, every time that happen, everyone ends up losing at the end. To elaborate, I would like to use the monetary system for my elaboration. For an example, Haiti interest, versus an individual or special group interest. I would like to use French for an example, let say the French feel bad about the state of Haiti and realizing collecting the money for recognizing our independence of Haiti as free country was wrong, and would like to return the money back to Haiti. Both the French and Haitians agree the value of the money is twenty billion dollars. The Haitian government collects the money and used the money for they own personal affairs, they have divide the money among each other, and they purchase big cars, big houses, and hide the rest in over sea bank, like Swiss bank, or bank of England or some French bank. As we, all know Haiti does not make any cars when those leaders bought nice expensive cars, they only help stimulate over sea economy. When they import materials from over sea to build nice expensive mansion, they only help stimulate over sea economy, worst of all, when their banking over sea, they help stimulate over sea markets instead of their own markets. As a result, over sea market would continue to increase while you continue to decreasing your own markets. Indeed, when your money hide in over seas bank, over sea people get to go to the bank, borrow your money, to open businesses, that create jobs for their own people in their own country. As your money creating jobs over sea, they would have better schools, better healthcare, better banking system, better government system, as those things occur, over sea currency will go up, while your currency will continuously to go down. For example, since they would have better government system, they will propose better legislation, to control the flow of money in order to prevent inflation and deflation of money in the markets; both inflation and deflation could affect the value of your currency. They would have the resources to propose better legislation for the private markets in order to prevent monopoly, any monopoly business is not good for the consumer, because company can increase or decrease the price as they please. The true price of a market is when company is competing among each other for your service. and they provide enough supply for the consumer demand, and as supply and demand are intersect, that would be the true cost the consumer will spend for that goods, without the proper resources, many country like Haiti do not have the capability to enforce any systematic market. As a result, they do not have control over their own economy. Indeed their currency would go down; as our currency is becoming worthless to the world, you and your people and your own country become worthless to the world. The best example, as I was watching the news on MSNBC, I saw the worse embarrass moment that could happen to any head of states; the president of Haiti Rene Preval, was trying to get the president of the United States Barrack Obama attention, he ignored Mr. preval like if he was nothing. Many people used the protocol excuse of why the president of United States ignores the president of Haiti; well, if that was the case at the same event, why didn't Mr. ob ignored Mr. Chavez the president of Venezuela, when he pulled him from the back, and try to give him his book that is criticize Mr. Obama own country. People have to understand, you represent what your country is represented, despite having all the money in the world, despite of what your status is, If you are a citizen of fail country, every buddy of the entire country is a failure, therefore, you, the citizens of your country and your country are all become irrelevant to the world.

In the other hand, let us say they want to be good leaders, and they want to use the money for Haiti interest. First, they would think what the best possible way to invest and create opportunity for the Haitians people. First, they would have to start to increase the security of the entire nation. Creating new bureaucracy of legitimate government program that oblige by the rules of law to the land and have to earn the legitimate trust of the entire Haitian people; then, that would create jobs in many aspects. First, we would have to train those new officers all over the entire country, as a result, we would created much jobs in the learning aspect and the training aspect, as we preparing those young Haitians men and women for duties. As a result, thousands of jobs would be create, while the entire population is being safer. Next, they would invest in energy, one of the biggest problem Haiti face is, is the fact we consume energy, but does not create or produce any kind of energy. According to world resources institute, in energy production and consumption, the direction Haiti is going compare to the Central America and the Caribbean is deplorable. To elaborate, Haiti profile in energy production and consumption in thousands metric tons of oil equivalent total energy production in 2000 was 1542 while Central America and the Caribbean produce 269834. Haiti has 18% decreased, while Central America and the Caribbean has 51% increase in energy production since 1980. In 1997, Haiti imported energy of 480 thousands metric tons of oil equivalent, while exported zero energy. Energy consumption per GDP in Haiti has increase up to 47% and central America and the Caribbean in between 1990 and 1999, Haiti has an increase of 47%, while central America and the Caribbean has decrease of consumption of 9% even the world has a decrease of energy of 13% of consumption between 1990 and 1999. It is clearly Haiti is going downward at a rapid pace, compare to our neighbor.

Indeed, it would have been one of the greatest invest toward our country, if our leaders would have invest toward energy production. Then, we would that energy to compete with the Chinese labor market. We would invest this energy in factories, agriculture, best of all, tourism, only those three markets can make a tremendous upward movement toward the Haitian economy over night; and it is almost impossible, for these markets to operate without both enough security and sufficient energy.

As a result, that would create the liberty we desperately need, and that would allow us the freedom to pursuit the happiness we have been thirst for over two centuries ago. Only then, this endless nightmare would end.

CHAPTER X

In my Haitian State of Mind.

It is clearly hates live here. Sometime I wonder, does hating someone or hating something is ever justifies. I was born in a country where mostly everyone who lives in the country hates the country. In fact, most us who live in the country would give up our entire life trying to make it out of the country if we could. Every time the Haitians trying to escape from Haiti and trying to go to any other destination beside Haiti, and each time I hear a Haitians boat sink into the ocean and there is no survivor remain, this is when I feel my deepest pain in my heart. A pain so deep I would not wish it to my worse enemy. In fact, those men and women who lost their lives usually left family behind; in return, those family ends up develop a deep kind of distress and dislike about Haiti. Never the less, how does an entire nation get to hate their entire country? They hate their entire country so much, anyone who trying to improve the situation, is in jeopardy of losing their lives. As a proud Haitian who lives both in Haiti and abroad, it is occurs to me that many Haitians, who live in Haiti, can visually see their misery in Haiti for an extremely long time. They can see the disparity in their children eyes, when sick and they cannot afford medical assistant. They can clear hear the echo inside their children stomachs pleading for food; and as a man and as father, the only thing you can do is to cover both ears. They can see their children seeing the hopeless in their eyes, and as a man and as a father, the only thing you can do is to cover your face for your children not see the shame in your face. The police, who risk their lives serving the country everyday, have to wait months and months before they can be paid for their hard work. A college graduate who turn to be a maid servant and encounter all kind of abuse from their boss, for just less than a dollar a day, and yet still have showed up everyday because this is the only thing that maintain her survival. Finally yet importantly, the young man I personally know, who graduated school 19 years ago, who has more than three college degrees, and yet to find a job to support himself and his family. As a result, knowing all these things about Haiti, I wonder if the strong hate my people have develop for our country is justify.

By living abroad, make me realize how contrary Haitians who live abroad are to the Haitians who live in Haiti. First, in a very short time the deepest hate we developed while we were living in Haiti, turn into the greatest love affair for Haiti. There could be a lot reason for such love affair. First, we have realized there are gloomy days everywhere you go in the world. Even countries that consider the best country in the world have their own tribulation and their own hardship. Just as in our country, they have homeless in the street begging for loose change, trying to feed their loves ones. Just as in our country, people still kill innocent civilian for their own persona property. Just as in our country, the law is blind to some part of their country. Just as in our country, it does not matter how hard you work, you may not still get that fair chance to spread your wings and fly. Most importantly, we have come to the realization that hope is the only light to darkness. One thing I realize living abroad that hope are dying in every corner in Haiti, as a result, progression have also die in every corner of Haiti. However, living abroad make us realize that we are not too far from those countries considering the best in the word. In fact, we have come to realize the possibilities to better our country are limitless. From being hopeless in our country, when we go abroad, some how hopes shine in all our heart about country. As a result, we have become much more patriotic of our country. The biggest obstacle we Haitians citizens abroad faced is that, we have yet to realize how to deliver our new found of hope to our people at home who live in the dark of disparity. Too often, we find it easy to sleep on hope and let hope die, rather, to engage our newfound obligation to spread our newfound hope to our country. Too often, hope die because of selfishness of human nature. The toxic selfish thinking we Haitians surrounding ourselves with, must be confront with unity in order to resolve the nation problems. The mentality, why make things harder for me in order to make thing easy for country is absurd in so many ways. Why help this Haitian man succeed when I am yet to be successful. If I am successful, why help this man succeed to be like me. Why let this man led even if I am not fit to lead, when I can be the leader forever. That kind of toxic thinking is among us all, it is a human character known as jealousy. This character come in different form and shape, The more educated you are about this character, the more aware of yourself you'll becoming, and the more self assure you will be about yourself, and the easy it would be to over come this deadly toxic character that seem to live in every Haitian mind especially our father generation.

As a Haitian citizen, I have come to realize it will take every Haitians citizen in the world to unit together for Haiti to see any strive toward progression. Especially the Haitians who live and travel over see, who is well educated around the world, and know the issues. The leaders in Haiti working extremely hard to shut the Haitians diasporas not to influence real change in Haiti, while they want us to continue help support the country. According to world statistics, and Diaspora organization, the Haitian Diaspora is one third of the country GDP. With that kind of support, we have the right to influence real change in Haiti. Haiti crisis is too big of crisis to exclude any group that is fighting for real change to better Haiti.

The Haitians leaders must understand what happen Haiti influence every Haitians in all parts of the world. It is in our both interest for Haiti to be successful. We the Diasporas would like to see peace and prosperity in Haiti. Most of us would not even dream of leaving our beautiful land, if we know we would have fair chance at life in Haiti. I could elaborate on so many things we miss from not being home. For example, we miss listen to the breeze of the ocean and the river. We miss waking up in the morning with the sound of the bird chanting to our backyard. We miss friends and loves we shared our firs kiss. We miss our favorite recipe to our favorite dish. Most of all, we miss the landscape of those beautiful mountain, as you drive through them that rush that you feel let you know you home. The thing we give up, when we leave home out weight any good, we receive elsewhere. It is imperil for Haitian Diaspora to continue not to have hand off attitude about the challenge Haiti face today. It would take all the Diasporas all over the world to go back to Haiti, and influence real changes in Haiti. It will take a great deal of sacrifice to leave your comfort zone to help your country, without a great deal of sacrifice from every Haitian, the people of Haiti, will get into a deeper hole. A hole as a nation we cannot afford to ignore any longer.

We must do this in the name of brotherly hood. It is occurs to me that evils are afraid of good. it does not matter how much evils someone is to doing to another, as long someone else is doing some good to combat that evil, the good will always prevail. My dream is for the Haitian Diasporas to continue to do good work to combat all those evil things that happening in Haiti. Too often, we assume sending a couple hundred dollars to our family in Haiti is good enough. Indeed, it is a temporary support, but we have to put more in consideration. It would be best to consider, an alternative solution, to fix the problems of what stopping our family from getting that couple hundreds to support themselves. As Haitians citizens living abroad, we have the luxury to know, all problems has a solution, instead of put a bandage into our problems, it will serve every buddy best by trying to solve the problems itself. Too often as nation, we settle for less. As a nation, in order for the nation, to reach its full potential, it requires everything we are not as nation. It is best that people of that nation to come together, and fight for common goal on how to uplift the country. The people of the nation must have an identity of what the country is stand for and against. The government of the country must have mutual respect for the people, vice versa. The people must respect and obey the law of the country. The law of the country must not be in favoritism of in individual or a special group, the law of any successful must be in the best interest of the public. Too often in Haiti, we do everything backwards, and expect to have an upwards solution. This kind of thinking is idiotic or childish at best. The fact is, you cannot cut the tree in front of your house, and expect for the tree to still standing in front of your house. If you careless about your government, the government will do less for the people as if we the Haitians need any proof. Unless we change our mind set as a nation, we will continue to fall behind the rest of the world. We are moving so far behind the world, we are exclusive our country from the world.

CHAPTER XI

Feeling Guilty of Living in America.

I am often amused by my own reactions when I realize how horrible my life is, and how there is not any friend in sight to rescued me from my misery. As a result, I usually start by blaming every friend for all the horrible things that usually happened in my life. First, I would go for days being mad. If someone would ask me, why am I so mad? More often, I would not know whom to blame. More often than not, being responsible for my own action, is still a learning process for me. However, even in good times, I wonder if I ever feel joy. When you were born in a country like a Haiti, which is one of the poorest countries in the world, coming to North America should bring you great joy. For many people that is often the case. As for me, it is a love and hate relation living my life in America. The same great beneficial things that I am grateful for in America, is the same great beneficial things that bring me a great deal of pain and suffering. The love and hate feelings begun in a warm Sunday morning November 16, 1996. it was a day that would live with me for as long as I am alive. I had a mixture of emotions that day. As you could imagine, spontaneously I was feeling joyful and sadness at the same time.

I was feeling joy, because growing up in Haiti you learned at an early age that every Haitian want to come to America and by having chance to come to America, was a dream come true. In addition, I was big fan of American culture. For example, their music, their sports, their movies, and most importantly, I was fascinating by their life stiles. Indeed, the myth that money grows in trees in America was enough to make you fly to America instantaneously. Moreover, it was impossible not to believe the mystery that money did grow in trees in America. Our fellow Haitians, who was dirt poor in Haiti, have gone to America and come back to Haiti, was now able to support his family and friends. Their children that was not able to school, now was in the best school in the country. Their children that didn't have any nice clothes, now was having the best clothes in the neighborhood. I for example, was living in nice neighborhood, six or seven bedroom apartment, attended nice school two three different car parking in the garage; and when I visit friends and family; it was just the opposite of our family live. The only thing that was different from my relative that my father was living in America, as a result, it was able to work and provide for his family, while some of my other relative didn't have the same chance.

Just like my father, many Haitians who come to America, help their immediate family. However, this is as far as it go. They don't remember the neighbor kids didn't no shoes last time their have visited Haiti. they don't remember the neighbor next door was not able to eat that Sunday morning after church; while we were throwing food away Monday morning. As you can clear see, very few of us do the right thing by helping friends and family. Most of us do not remember if they were in the same position a year ago. They developed amnesia in short period of time. Prior to America, these Haitian were caring and sharing for each other. They respected each other. In a very short run, all those great characters from these Haitian seem to disappear. Now, they become obnoxious. Before I came to America, I did not understand the sudden change about these Haitians. My first reaction was to blame the Americans. However, after coming to America, I have realized, America was not to be blame. First, when most Haitians move up a class in society, their main intention, is to keep the ones at the bottom to drop lower at bottom of the pile. They would go out of their way to make it impossible for you to move up. To illustrate, many Haitian go frequently back to Haiti, when passing through the American airports, there would be any difficulties, however, I cant say the same for the Haitians airports. If you lose weight and you look slight different from your passport, or your paper work you would be question; and you without a doubt, you would be delay possibly miss your fliht from the Haitian airport.

To be truthfully, I do not think my people like to see each other be successful. Even this issue victimized me, when my sister was getting straight A's in school, I was very jealous of her. It was not as if I was not capable of making straight A's in school, I was too jealous of grades, I waist all my energy being jealous rather using the same strategy she used to get straight A's. as I got wised up, I stop being jealous, and focus on what she was doing to get those good grades, which was study hard, all the sudden, we both was making straight A's. as a result, we all successful in our education.

I am afraid, this is the lesson my Haitian people is not learning as a nation. We need to be more complimentary to each other. We need to be more respectful to each other. We need to value our country. In order to have a better country, first we have to better ourselves first as individual, and as a whole; because believe or not, without any doubt, Haiti is one of the best country in the world. Our music, our beauty, our history, our resilience, our compassion, they would come to life only if we unit and love one another as an individual most importantly as a nation.

www.ingramcontent.com/pod-product-compliance
Lightning Source LLC
Chambersburg PA
CBHW050340290526
45785CB00006B/2573